Italian Riviera & Cinque Terre Travel Guide

Attractions, Eating, Drinking, Shopping & Places To Stay

Sharon Hammond

Copyright © 2015, Astute Press
All Rights Reserved.

No part of this publication may be reproduced, stored in a retrieval system, or transmitted, in any form or by any means without the prior written permission of the publisher, nor be otherwise circulated in any form of binding or cover other than that in which it is published and without similar condition being imposed on the subsequent purchaser.

If there are any errors or omissions in copyright acknowledgements the publisher will be pleased to insert the appropriate acknowledgement in any subsequent printing of this publication.

Although we have taken all reasonable care in researching this book we make no warranty about the accuracy or completeness of its content and disclaim all liability arising from its use

Table of Contents

Italian Riviera 2
  Culture 2
  Location & Orientation 2
  Climate & When to Visit..3

Sightseeing Highlights 4
  A Walk around Genoa 4
    Via Garibaldi 4
    Mura della citta..4
    Church of San Siro 4
    Galata Museo del Mare 4
    Felice Ippolito National Antarctic Museum.......................5
    Museum of Etnomedicine "Antonio Scarpa"....................5
    Museum of Oriental Art Edoardo Chiossone 5
  Portofino 5
    Cristo degli Abissi (Christ of the Abyss) 5
  Camogli 5
  Alassio 5
  Cinque Terre 6
  Balzi Rossi Caves & the Museum of Prehistory 6
  Roman Ruins in the Italian Riviera 6
  The Gulf of Poets, La Spezia 6
  Sanremo...7
    Bussana Vecchia 7
  Hanbury Botanical Garden...7
  Dolceacqua...7

Recommendations for the Budget Traveller....................8
  Places to Stay...8
    Agririfugio Molini 8
    Hotel Eden 8
    Hotel Maristella 8
    Grand Hotel Des Anglais 8
    Hotel Cairoli 8
  Places to Eat...8
    Cocoon 8
    Ristorante Il Gambero Rosso...9

Nuovo Piccolo Mondo 9
Le Rune..9
La Cantina del Pescatore 9

Places to Shop 9
Galleria Umberto...9
Five Stones...9
Markets in Liguria 9
Victoria..9
Discounted Fashion Outlets 9

Cinque Terre...11

Planning Your Stay 11

Climate & Weather 11

Sightseeing 11

Riomaggiore 11
Church of Saint John the Baptist...11
Other Churches & Devotional Sites 11
Castle of Riomaggiore 11

Manarola 11
Church of San Lorenzo...11

Corniglia 11
Church of San Pietro 11
Largo Taragio...11
Oratory of the Disciplinati of Saint Catherine........................11
San Bernardino 11
Guvano Beach 11

Vernazza..11
Voluntourism in Vernazza 11

Monterosso del Mar 11
Il Gigante..11
Monastery of the Capuchin Friars of Monterosso del Mar...........11
Dawn Tower (Torre Aurora) 11

Hiking in Cinque Terre...11
The Blue Trail (Trail Number 2)...11
Via Dell'Amore 11
From Manarola to Monterosso 11
The Five Sanctuaries Trail..11
Cinque Terre High Trail (Trail Number 1)..............................11

Wine Tour of Cinque Terre 11

Recommendations for the Budget Traveller 11

Shopping 11
Cantina du Sciacchetra 11
Enoteca Internazionale 11
Enoteca Sotto l'Arco 11
Il Mercante d'Oriente 11
Galleria D'Arte Schiaccheart 11

Places to Stay 11
Hotel Villa Steno 11
La Marina Rooms 11
Il Carugio di Corniglia 11
Arpaiu 11
Alla Marina 11

Eating & Drinking 11
Enoteca da Eliseo (Wine Bar) 11
Il Casello 11
Il Pirata delle Cinque Terre 11
Marina Piccola's Ristorante Albergo Sul Mare 11
Il Borgo di Campi 11

Italian Riviera

The Italian Riviera is nestled between the French Riviera, Monaco and Tuscany on the Ligurian coast. Genoa was the birthplace of Christopher Columbus while Portofino attracts the rich and famous to its beautiful marina.

There are two faces to the Italian Riviera. East, towards the rising sun, is the Riviera of Palms. The western arm of the coastal region is known as Riviera dei Fiori, as it is home to a lucrative flower industry.

Notable visitors ranged from the English poets Shelly and Lord Byron to D.H. Lawrence and Ernest Hemingway and later, Hollywood celebrities such as Elizabeth Taylor and Ava Gardner. Another famous figure from the past, born in Genoa, was violinist Nicolo Paganini.

Liguria has a narrow strip of habitable terrain that is situated between the land and sea. The beautiful pastel-hued buildings and quaint and historical harbors are set against dramatic rock features. While towns like Portofino and the villages of the Cinque Terre are immensely popular for their quaint charm, they remain small and can get extremely crowded at the height of the summer season. Sanremo (also referred to as San Remo) to the west is somewhat larger and better developed as a holiday destination. Even in cities such as Genoa, many of the historical streets are narrow and feature lots of architectural splendor.

Thanks to the mostly pleasant climate and plenty of natural shelter in the form of caves, the Italian Riviera has revealed rich finds of prehistoric remains ranging from cave art, fossils of hominids such as Cro-Magnon and the Neanderthal Man and also bones suggestive of a great diversity of animal life, some of which are no longer native to the region.

Genoa was first settled in the 4th century BC and served as port and gateway to the northern parts of Italy from the earliest part of its history. In medieval times and after, it developed to a powerful city-state, but during the 19th century, this city's people led the path towards Italy's unification.

Culture

In some parts of the Italian Riviera, human settlement dates back to prehistoric times. The Roman Empire left its mark and early conversion to Christianity birthed a new culture of churches that grew from humble communities to impressive Romanesque and Gothic structures. Yet, the geographic limitations of mountain and sea left little room for large cities to develop and instead the area drew the independent thinkers, the artists and the poets.

Perhaps due to the region's isolation from the rest of Italy, the people of Liguria have a reputation for being somewhat aloof towards outsiders. Throughout the ages, its capital, Genoa has embraced new ideals, whether positive, such as monetary relief for the poor or negative, in the form of Fascism. Self-determination has always been the motivating factor of the region. After a railway system rendered the Italian Riviera more accessible to the outside world, it became a fashionable holiday destination with towns like Portofino emerging as a favorite of the rich and the beautiful.

The city of Genoa hosts an annual violin competition of international calibre in honor of Nicolo Paganini. It takes place in September through to October. A prominent 20th century representative of the Ligurian music scene is singer-songwriter, Fabrizio de Andrè. The cuisine is typically mediterranean, with pasta, seafood and olive oil featuring prominently and the region is well known for producing olive oil and wine.

Location & Orientation

The Italian Riviera is a name often used to describe the coastal region known as Liguria. It lies sandwiched between the natural boundaries of the Alps, the Apennines Mountains and the Ligurian Sea. The region is geographically isolated and some of its villages were until relatively recent times only accessible by boat.

About two thirds of the terrain is quite mountainous and at least 12 percent is made up of natural reserves. Liguria is subdivided into four provinces, namely Imperia, Savona, Genoa and La Spezia. Genoa, the region's capital is centrally located. The western Riviera is well known for its flower industry, while the east is more rugged.

Water traffic once played a large role in connecting the little villages of the Italian Riviera and is still frequently used as some of the more remote settlements are easier to reach that way. There is a coastal road and rail network. If you are planning to use some of the region's popular hiking trails, bear in mind that they are sometimes steep and physically demanding.

There is an airport that services Genoa, but if you are travelling to the western towns of the Italian Riviera, Nice might be a more convenient terminal.

Climate & When to Visit

The combination of mountain and sea does allow for the creation of numerous microclimates.

Rainfall can vary. Genoa, for example, can typically experience up to 2000mm of rain annually, while other towns might only achieve an average of between 500 and 800mm. The summer day temperatures of Genoa average between 27 and 28 degrees Celsius, with night temperatures staying fairly high at around 28 degrees Celsius. In the winter months, temperatures fluctuate between 11 degrees Celsius in the day and 6 degrees Celsius at night. You can still expect maximum temperatures in the low twenties in the months of May, September and October.

San Remo, a popular resort town in the west, enjoys mild weather throughout the year. In the warmest months of July and August, you can expect average highs of around 27 degrees Celsius, with night temperatures typically dropping to around 20 degrees Celsius. In January the average temperature fluctuates between a daytime temperature of around 13 degrees Celsius, with a nocturnal drop to around 6 degrees Celsius. The months of May, September and October still enjoy average highs above 20 degrees Celsius. This area sees an annual rainfall of 700mm, with the bulk of it falling in November. July sees the least rainfall per year.

Sightseeing Highlights

A Walk around Genoa

Via Garibaldi

West of Piazza Fontane Marose,
Maddalena, Genoa, Italy

When exploring the historical center of Genoa, an impressive sight is Via Garibaldi. This narrow, cobblestone street, barely 7.5m wide and 250m long, dates back to 1550, when it was known by the original name of Strada Maggiore.

What makes it remarkable, is the opulent palaces of yesteryear that occupy the area within its confines.

The most impressive of these are Palazzo Rosso, Palazzo Bianco and Palazzo Doria Tursi, three mansions are collectively known as Musei di Strada Nuova. Before the street was renamed to honor Garibaldi's contribution to Italy, the street had for a period been known as Strada Nuova. Palazzo Rossa or the Red Palace was constructed in the 1670s according to the plans of Pietro Antonio. Once the property of the Brignole-Sale family, it was bequeathed to the city of Genoa in 1874, along with a substantial collection of art, which includes paintings by Albrecht Dürer, Van Dyck, Guido Reni, Paolo Veronese, Bernardo Strozzi and Guercino.

Palazzo Bianco or the White Palace is the repository of a similarly striking series of exhibits. Some of the artists represented include Rubens, Jean Provost, Caravaggio, Hans Memling, Murillo, Francisco de Zurbarán, Magnasco, Bernardo Strozzi, Van Dyck, Nicolas Lancret and many more. Dating back to 1540, it is even older than Palazzo Rosso.

Palazzo Doria-Tursi features a treasure of a different kind - a violin created by the master luthier Giuseppe Guarneri that had been gifted to Nicolo Paganini by a wealthy admirer. Paganini was born in Genoa in 1782. The palace also boasts a collection of decorative art, coins and the weights and measures of commerce. Palazzo Doria-Tursi is also used for official business by the mayor and City Council of Genoa.

Some of the other palaces worth a visit are Palazzo Mediana, which features a sundial in its facade, Palazzo Cambiaso and Palazzo Gambaro. The street has been declared a UNESCO World Heritage Site.

Mura della citta

Via Tommaso Reggio, Castelleto, 16136 Genoa, Italy
(Piazza De Ferrari)

As an important port, Genoa has enjoyed the benefit of solid fortification from early times. While Mura della cita does not quite match the Great Wall of China, it is acknowledged to be Europe's longest wall, measuring a total of 13km. Sections of the wall date all the way back to the 12th century. Some re-enforcement and expansion occurred over time, most notably in the 17th century when Genoa had to withstand an attack from the Duke of Savoy. During this period the portion known as the New Wall was added.

The medieval gate of Porta Soprana survives, squeezed between two imposing towers. The western gate of Porta dei Vacca, dating back to 1155, is likewise still functional, but a third gate, the so-called 'Golden Gate' or Porta Aurea was demolished in the 1800s.

Each portion of the wall once had a separate name ascribed to its bastion, although some of these are now illegible and lost. The view of Genoa from the fort at the top is awe-inspiring but bear in mind that the path is long and steep. Parco delle Mura surrounds the area with over 600 hectares of natural vegetation and wildlife.

Church of San Siro

Via San Luca, Maddalena, Genoa, Italy (Righi)
Tel: 010 22461468

Located near Via Garibaldi in the historical center of Genoa, the Church of San Siro was constructed in the 4th century. It is the oldest church in Genoa and its ancient predecessor had been dedicated to the Apostles. The current building is named after a bishop from the 6th century.

During the 11th century, it came into the care of the Benedictines. The building gained prominence as the seat of Genoa's bishop and was re-modelled to the Romanesque style of that era. Fire in the 15th century necessitated more rebuilding. More restoration occurred in the 17th and 19th century.

Galata Museo del Mare

Calata De Mari, 1, Genoa, Italy
Tel: 010 2345 655
http://www.galatamuseodelmare.it/jsp/index.jsp

Genoa boasts a proud maritime history and if you wish to learn a little more of it, do pay a visit to its maritime museum.

There are various models of boats, including a life size replica of a 16th century galley ship and a submarine. Special attention is paid to one of the most famous figures of Genoa's seafaring tradition, Christopher Columbus. Some of the exhibits include authentic correspondence by the man who discovered the Americas, but there are also smaller models of ships and numerous maps and charts.

Felice Ippolito National Antarctic Museum

Palazzina Millo
Area Expo' Porto Antico, Genoa
Tel: 010 2543690

This museum showcases several specimens of flora and fauna brought back by Italian explorers from the Antarctic.

Museum of Etnomedicine "Antonio Scarpa"

University of Genoa,
Department of Anthropological Sciences,
Via Balbi 4, Genoa
Tel 010 2095044

This speciality museum includes various objects, instruments and artefacts from the collection of Antonio Scarpa. There is a general theme of healing and medicine. There is no charge.

Museum of Oriental Art Edoardo Chiossone

Villetta Dinegro, Piazzale Mazzini, 4 - 16122 Genova
Tel: 010 542285

This extensive museum contains the personal collection of Edoardo Chiossone, artist and a native of Genoa who spent many years in Japan. It features a large selection of Oriental art objects.

Portofino

The name Portofino originated with the Latin 'Portus Delphini' which means Port of Dolphins.

Since the time of Pliny the Elder, dolphins had been observed off the coast of Portofino.

During the 1950s and 1960s, Portofino rose to unexpected prominence when it came to be frequented by a number of celebrities such as Frank Sinatra, Elizabeth Taylor, Brigitte Bardot, Ingrid Bergman and Ernest Hemingway. The actor Sir Rex Harrison owns a villa here. Even today, it is still a great town for star spotting as more recent high profile visitors include Kylie Minogue, Leonardo di Caprio, Rihanna and Jennifer Lopez.

Portofino offers plenty of opportunity for exploration, via hiking routes, through boat trips or by scuba diving off the coast to explore its fascinating underwater scenery and life forms.

A gorgeous place to visit in Portofino is the sculpture garden at Museo del Parco. It occupies grounds that once belonged to Baron von Mumm and shows sculptures by artists such as Man Ray, Arman, Alberto Burri and Pietro Consagra within a natural outdoor setting. The present curator of this unusual collection is Daniele Crippa.

Cristo degli Abissi (Christ of the Abyss)

The Bay of Portofino

One of the more unusual attractions of Portofino is the statue known as Christ of the Abyss. Sculpted by Guido Galletti and inspired by a concept of Duilo Marcante, this monument occupies a spot on the seabed in the bay of Portofino, 17m below the surface of the water.

Duilo Marcante, a native of Genoa, had been an enthusiastic diver from the 1930s. He pioneered many diving innovations and grew to prominence in scuba diving circles through his association with the Underwater Center in Nervi. He introduced training methods employed by fire-fighters to diving tuition and one of his more significant ideas involved strategies to accommodate water pressure on the eardrum in order to minimize potential damage. Marcante wrote a training manual, two books and a number of articles on the subject.

The statue, Christ of the Abyss, was dedicated to Dario Gonzatti, a personal friend of Duilo Marcante, who had died during an underwater excursion. It was created free of charge to facilitate a place of devotion and prayer for divers and fishermen within the depths of the ocean. Cristo degli Abissi or Christ of the Abyss had been inaugurated on 29 August 1954.

Camogli

Camogli is located near Portofino, but is somewhat less developed than its more popular neighbor. The village features a small fishing port and a colorful array of houses adorning its rocky landscape. Its main architectural sights include the most prominent church, the Basilica Santa Maria Assunta and Castello Dragonara, the town's fortress against pirate attack. Interestingly, the fort also houses an aquarium in olden times.

Camogli can be used as a base from which to explore Portofino or the nearby San Fruttuoso abbey. Some of its features include an oval shaped dome and its most ancient section, the belfry. The hike towards the small settlement is steep and quite challenging. The easier way of reaching San Fruttuoso is by boat.

Alassio

The town of Alassio dates back to the year 1000. A romantic legend has it that the town was founded by a Saxon princess Adelasia who had eloped with her lover Aleramo. A more likely explanation would be that settlers simply saw the early advantages of its sheltered bay for sea trade. Over the years, it had fallen under the control of the religious community at Gallinara, Albenga, Genoa, Sardinia and Italy.

The town withstood Barbary raiders during the turbulent 16th century, thanks to the vigilant presence of Torrione della Coscia or the watchtower, which can still be admired today. The Tower of Vegliasco dates back to the year 967 and is associated with the Aleramo family.

The 19th century brought an unexpected period of prosperity, when various artists, writers, poets and other creative individuals discovered the Italian Riviera. Some were particularly drawn to Alassio. Edward Elgar composed an overture in its honor. When a railway line was completed in 1872, more visitors arrived. World War Two briefly damped the atmosphere, but from the 1950s, a new generation of celebrities were drawn to its shores, particularly with the advent of the famous performance venue, Cafe Roma. The author Ernest Hemingway was an early patron, but other visitors include Italian celebrities such as Mina, Domenico Modugno and the racer Valentino Rossi.

The island Gallinara lies off the coast near Albenga and Alassio. Once it had been the refuge of Martin of Tours, a hermit and saint from the 4th century. Later a Benedictine monastery was founded here. Today, the area is a protected reserve for cliff-dwelling herring gulls.

Alassio has several religious buildings of interest. The Church of St Ambrogio at Via Mazzini 3 was built in the 15th century, but an earlier church dating back to the 10th century had previously occupied the site.
Administratively, the hilltop village of Solva forms part of Alassio. Its 15th century church, Santissima Annunziata is worth a visit for its well-preserved frescoes. The church at Cape Santa Croce goes back to the 12th century.

To the east, you will find the marina with a Cappelletta to honor fallen Marines. The beach is popular with tourists and is lined by a marine promenade. Parallel to the length of the coast, in the historical district, you will find the Budello, a narrow, ancient alley or carruggio that will take you to several buildings dating back to the 1500s and 1600s, but also various shops and workshops.

One fun way to experience Alassio is via a historical train route that lasts half an hour and costs €4. The spa at Alassio is slightly pricey, but includes use of a saltwater pool, Turkish baths, sauna, ice fountain and access to various water based and beauty treatments.

Cinque Terre

One of the top ranking attractions of the Italian Riviera is the region known as Cinque Terre. The name translates to 'five lands', referring to the five interlinked villages that make up the Cinque Terre. These are Riomaggiore and Manarola to the south, the middle village Corniglia, which is also the highest and Vernazza and Monterosso al Mar. Declared a UNESCO Heritage Site in 1997, the villages remain largely unspoilt by modern development. The only one that has taken some of the features of a resort town is Monterosso.

A popular hiking trail links all five villages, but this can be challenging in part, particularly the latter part of the route to Corniglia, which perches on a hill and is accessible via 365 steps.

The less active tourist may be relieved to learn that this beautiful village can also be reached by bus. A feature of Corniglia's piazza is a communal olive press. A similarly steep descent will bring you from Corniglia to Vernazza. Notable features of Vernazza are its attractive cove, a pirate's lookout tower and its decorative pastel-colored houses.

The easiest walk is Via del Amore, which has a romantic reputation for connecting would-be lovers of the towns Riomaggiore and Manarola. This forms part of the greater coastal or Blue Route. Admittance is €3.00. The route crosses flat terrain, covers about 850m and should not take longer than 25 minutes. There are checkpoints along the way, and a small cafe, Bar dell Amore, which serves refreshments. There is a tradition for young lovers to inscribe their names on a padlock and then lock this symbolic emblem of their devotion for each other to the wire mesh found along the trail.

Two well-known wines are native to this region, the dry white-labelled *Cinque Terre* and the somewhat sweeter dessert wine called *Sciacchetra*. Olives, figs and lemons are also grown here and Monterosso hosts an annual Lemon Festival.

Manarola is a quintessential fishing village with an extensive fleets of boats found along its pier. There are also interesting underwater caves and rock features to explore.

Balzi Rossi Caves & the Museum of Prehistory

The Balzi Rossi or 'Red' caves has been the repository of a rich collection of animal fossils as well as early stone tools. The site is located 7km west of Ventimiglia and close to the French border. Its existence had been known since the 18th century and joint excavations sponsored by the French and Italian government revealed that a variety of life had flourished here during various periods. The remains of animals as diverse as reindeer and elephants have been dug up.

Some of the human remains have been classified as Grimaldi Man, while others were associated with the Cro Magnon. Various examples of prehistoric art have also been uncovered. These include figurines, sculpted rock as well as paintings. A museum created by Sir Thomas Hanbury displays artefacts and fossils from the site. The site can be accessed via Motorway A10 or A8, or by using a bus service from Ventimiglia.

Roman Ruins in the Italian Riviera

Museo archeologico nazionale di Luni
Via Luni, 37, 19034 Ortonovo
Province of La Spezia, Italy

There are settlements in Liguria that date back to the Roman era and some of these still have ruins that are worth a visit.

Luni or Luna, to use its older name, lies along the shores of the River Magra and the bay of La Spezie has been identified as Portus Lunae, its trade outlet.

In 177 BC, Luni was used as a base from which the Ligurian coast was administered. Various contemporary sources refer to its existence, Pliny commented favorably on the quality of its cheeses and its marble was used in several Roman works. Later, it became a center for Liguria's new Christian converts.

Excavations begun in the 18th and 19th century and continued in the 1950s reveal some of the story of this fascinating city of the past. The ruins of two temples, a forum, an amphitheatre and various houses with notable artwork have been uncovered. Some of the finds, which includes pottery, coins and other artefacts can be viewed at the Museo archeologico nazionale di Luni or National Archaeological Museum of Luni, which is located at the site.

Another town with important Roman remains is Vertimiglia. An archaeological site reveals the excavated ruins of thermal baths and a Roman Theatre. In ancient times, it had belonged to the city of Albintimilium. Albenga too has a number of Roman finds located within its museums. The Palazzo Peloso Cepolla contains the Roman Ship Museum, whereas the Ingauno Museum displays urns and stone fragments associated with Roman and Byzantine settlement.

Taggia had been an important Roman settlement, but it also features tombs dating back to 700 BC and earlier. Under Rome it served as a port called Costa Balenae.

The Gulf of Poets, La Spezia

The Gulf of La Spezia is often referred to by another name - the Gulf of Poets - as several well-known poets were inspired by its ruggedly dramatic landscape. George Gordon Byron, better known simply as Lord Byron, lived in Portovenere and was a close friend of Percy Bysshe Shelly, who was based in San Terenzo. Grotto Arpaia is associated with Lord Byron. According to one anecdote, the poet once swam from Portovenere, where he lived to Lerici to visit the Shelleys.

Other famous literati developed a fondness for the region were D H Lawrence, Virginia Woolf, George Sand and a number of Italian wordsmiths such as Petrarca, Montale, Gabriele D'Annunzio and Filippo Tommaso Marinetti. The first to coin the phrase, though, was allegedly the Italian dramatist Sem Benelli.

There are several islands nearby, namely Palmaria, Tino and Tinetto and some of the beautiful villages, such as Fezzano, La Grazie, La Serra and Tellaro are worth a visit for their sheer beauty. D H Lawrence lived in Fiascherino. Portovenere, once Portus Veneris, dates back to the first century before Christ. Its San Pietro Church now occupies the same site once reserved for an ancient temple to Venus.

Sanremo

Located only 25km from the French border and approximately 60km from the airport in Nice, Sanremo is often referred to as the Flower Capital of Europe. The shelter offered by surrounding hills and mountains as well as the moderating influence of the sea combine to create a microclimate that is ideal for the large-scale cultivation of flowers. This is one of Sanremo's main industries and the town is home to a very active international market in flowers.

Originally founded to buffer the population against raids of piracy, Sanremo developed into a fashionable holiday destination. The town was a favorite of wealthy Russians, leading to the construction of a Russian Orthodox Church in 1913. Even before that time, in 1905, it gained another attraction - the casino. Completed in 1905, Sanremo Casino is the oldest establishment of its kind in Italy. Besides gambling, the venue also has an entertainment theatre, a restaurant, Biribissi and an attractive Roof Garden.

Sanremo hosts a variety of special events throughout the year. The casino sees a whole calendar of symphonic events, and there are several other musical events in Sanremo throughout the year, such as an International Song Festival in March, a Rock Festival in July and a Jazz Festival in August. There is a flower parade, water sports events as well as a cycling race from Milan to Sanremo.

The historical center of Sanremo is known as La Pigna, or "the pine cone", a maze of narrow, cobblestone alleys dating back to medieval times. Ascending to the highest point will give you an amazing view of the port and town below. Here, too, you will find the Gardens of Queen Elena and the Madonna della Costa Sanctuary, which dates back to the 17th century.

Bussana Vecchia

Located within the municipal boundaries of San Remo, Bussana Veccia was founded around 1050, as a hilltop refuge against repeated Saracen attack. It flourished during the 15th century, but fell to the unexpected catastrophe of an earthquake estimated between 6.2 and 6.5 on the Richter scale. This occurred on 23rd February 1887. The event killed around 2000 people throughout Liguria, but its impact on Bussana Vecchia was devastating and the village was abandoned.

Soon after the end of World War Two, illegal squatters began to occupy some of the remaining structures. Police tried to combat this development, but during the 1960s the ghost village attracted different types of settlers - artistic hippies from all over Europe who wished to live simply and close to nature.

Today the site boasts several studios, a few restaurants and pubs and even a bed and breakfast establishment. In the early years, the community had to do without basic services such as electricity, water and sanitation, but these days a section of the village had been connected to the municipal power grid. Some of the resident crafters include Studio W+J, the oldest of its kind, Studio Wilmot, which features the art of Colin Wilmot, La Bilancia, which showcases the art of Antonio di Michele and the work of Silvano Manco at Studio Manco. The eatery, Ristorante Naturale uses freshly grown organic produce in all their meals.

Hanbury Botanical Garden

Sir Thomas Hanbury spent the first twenty years of his adult life amassing a fortune in the Shanghai tea trade. From China, he relocated to the village La Mortola, on the Italian Riviera, where he was to create his most memorable legacy to mankind, the Hanbury Botanical Garden. He devoted four decades until his death in 1907 to this pursuit.

Sir Thomas shared his love of gardening with his brother Daniel, a notable botanist who took an active interest in his project. Sir Thomas Hanbury's daughter in law, Lady Dorothy Hanbury continued his work, but unfortunately the destruction of World War Two left its mark on the garden. The garden was eventually acquired by the University of Genoa. Considerable effort has been made towards its restoration.

The Hanbury Botanical Gardens is located near the town of Ventimiglia and now occupies 18 hectares of land. There are different color-coded hiking routes to follow through the garden and, besides over 5,800 plant species you will also encounter features such as fountains and sculptures along the way. Near Hanbury Villa, there is a Japanese bell dating back to 1764 and a mosaic honoring Marco Polo. The garden includes an orchard of rare fruit trees, such as the feijoa or pineapple guava and the Diospyros or persimmon, the carica or papaya.

Dolceacqua

The medieval village of Dolceacqua is as pretty as a painting, and features in several works by the impressionist artist Claude Monet, who lived nearby. The area is rich in flowers and has lots of character. One of the most distinctive views of the town is that of the humped stone bridge that spans the River Nervia, linking the more ancient Terra district with the relatively newer development of Borgo. Near the old bridge, lies the Church of San Filippo.

The village came into the ownership of the powerful Doria family in the mid-13th century, having previously fallen within the domain of the Ventimiglia nobles. Its oldest place of worship is the Romanesque styled parish church of San Giorgio, which dates back to the 12th century and includes the graves of Stefano and Julius Doria within its crypt. Periodic restorations account for Dolceacqua's many Gothic and Baroque features.

The medieval castle is now a ruin, although its towers are still clearly visible. Dolceacqua's convent had once been a prominent Benedictine priory and also an important point on a historic route that connected the Ligurian coastal settlements with the Alps. Archaeological finds in the locality of San Bernardo suggest that the settlement once enjoyed a strong connection with the Celtic people and tradition. The region is known for the olives and the wine it produces.

Recommendations for the Budget Traveller

Places to Stay

Agririfugio Molini

Loc. Molini di San Fruttuoso, 16032 Camogli, Italy

If you are looking for a peaceful yet picturesque stay in the Italian Riviera, do consider a stay in the beautiful fishing town Camogli.

Located roughly 8km west of Portofino and 22km east of Genoa, it can provide a convenient, yet affordable base. Agririfugio Molini nestles on a hillside that provides a beautiful view of the San Fruttuouso bay and the nearby abbey, but may best suit visitors that are fit and able as the path is slightly steep. The atmosphere is semi-rural, but facilities do include high-speed Internet and service is friendly. Accommodation begins at €44 and includes breakfast.

Hotel Eden

Via Dritto, 18, 16034 Portofino, Italy

Due to its trendy reputation, accommodation in Portofino can seem a little pricey. By these standards, Hotel Eden would appear affordable. The rooms are quite small, but includes a TV, a safe, free Wifi access and are well maintained. Accommodation begins at €112 a night and includes breakfast. Bear in mind that peak season rates in Portofino can rise quite steeply.

Hotel Maristella

Corso Imperatrice, 77, 18038 Sanremo, Italy

Located on the western section of the Italian Riviera, Sanremo makes a convenient base from which to explore the Flower Riviera and its surrounds and venture further afield.

 Hotel Maristella provides few frills, but rooms are well serviced. The terrace with loungers provides a great area for relaxation. Although rates are affordable at €62 per night, few extras are available without extra payment. A good breakfast is included in the price, but Wifi is extra.

Grand Hotel Des Anglais

Salita Grande Albergo, 8, Corso Imperatrice, 18038 Sanremo, Italy

The hotel evokes a vintage atmosphere, as the building dates back to the mid to late 1800s. It is conveniently located near the city center and rooms include a safe, flat-screen satellite TV, a mini-bar, shower and free high speed Internet. The staff is described as friendly and rooms are large and comfortable. The price begins at €52 per night and includes breakfast.

Hotel Cairoli

Via Cairoli 14/4, 16124 Genoa, Italy (Castelletto)
Tel: 010 246 1454
http://www.hotelcairoligenova.com/en/

Located within the historical section of Genoa, Hotel Cairoli combines a bright and rather modern looking decor based on various works of contemporary artistic expression with good old family care.

All rooms include a safe, satellite TV, a mini-bar, a safe and free Wifi Internet. The hotel features a reading room and a bar and breakfast is included in the price. Accommodation begins at €60 a night, but a minimum stay of two nights is imposed.

Places to Eat

Cocoon

Via Cavour, 24, 18038 San Remo, Italy
Tel: 390184610772
http://www.cocoonbar.com/cocoonbar.com/Home.html

Apart from a range of coffees and cocktails, Cocoon also offers a range of salads and sandwiches. The Club sandwich, which costs €6, is highly recommended. The eatery also features cupcakes and muffins. Although the food is fairly basic, it is well prepared.

The restaurant also offers a tapas selection. It is a Wifi free zone. Cocoon is open for breakfast and lunch. Salads are priced between €6.50 and €8, while the burgers are between €5 and €5.50.

Ristorante Il Gambero Rosso

Piazza Marconi n.7, 19018 Vernazza, Italy
Tel: 0187 812265

After you have feasted your eyes on the beautiful scenery of Vernazza and its surroundings, you may want to enjoy a taste of its flavorful traditional cuisine as well.

The menu features a great selection of pasta dishes, many with seafood, but they do include a few meat dishes. Appetizers vary between €12 and €18, with mains costing between €14 and €25. There is also a selection of sweets, prices at €6.

Nuovo Piccolo Mondo

Piave 7, 18038 Sanremo, Italy
Tel: 0184 509012

A favorite with locals in Sanremo, Nuovo Piccolo Mondo displays a retro 1920s exterior and offers delicious food at affordable prices. Included on the menu are Ligurian specialities such as stewed octopus with potatoes and pannacotta. There are a variety of pasta choices such as penne arrabiatta and spaghetti piccolo mondo. Management does speak English. Expect to pay around €50 for a meal for two with wine included.

Le Rune

Vico Domoculta, 14, 16100 Genoa, Italy (Piccapietra)
Tel: 010 594951

Tucked away in an inconspicuous setting, Le Rune is one of Genoa's delightful culinary discoveries. The menu features a variety of creative and original items such as lasagne with burrata, lobster risotto, ravioli with rabbit meat and mushrooms, timballo di robiola with a pear and cinnamon sauce and the tagliata di tonno with a fennel and grapefruit sauce. Expect to pay between €30 and €35 for a full meal excluding the wine. A lighter menu is available, with meals ranged between €21 and €28.

La Cantina del Pescatore

via V Emanuele 19, Monterosso al Mare, Italy

The cuisine of the Cinque Terre region is often described as extremely tasteful. If you wish to experience some of it, do pay a visit to La Cantina del Pescatore. There is an inside and outside area and the coffee is highly recommended. On the menu, you can expect pasta dishes, bruschettas, salad and panna. Do try the limoncello, which is a famous lemon liqueur. The restaurant also offers free Wifi. Expect to pay between €6 and €15.

Places to Shop

Galleria Umberto

Via Roma, Between Piazza de Ferrari and Piazza Corvetto
Genoa

The shopping mall known as Galleria Umberto dates back to the 1880s and besides the usual shops, it also provides space to a large bustling flea market. If you are looking for antiques or just curiosities from yesteryear, this is a great place to browse for bargains.

Five Stones

Halfway between Corniglia and Vernazza
Cinque Terre
Tel: 3480 459085
http://fivestones.yolasite.com/

If you are visiting the Cinque Terre region, you may wish to stop at a souvenir shop with a difference. Everything at five stones is made of natural resources such as stone, wood, cork, twigs, twine or paper. Everything on sale is hand made through the creative combination of complimentary elements.

Markets in Liguria

As with most regions of the Mediterranean, many of the towns and villages of Liguria have regular flea markets or craft markets, where dedicated browsers could pick up a bargain or two. Even Genoa has a small antique market of about 80 stalls on the first Saturday of the month, located at Palazzo Ducale. Chiavari's antique market is slightly larger, with over 100 stalls trading on the second Sunday and third Saturday at Via Martiri della Lliberazione e Caruggio Drito. Calizzano and Sassello host annual antique markets in August. There are also a number of markets in the area that sell handcrafted items. The market in Savona's historical center is known for its reasonably priced ceramic items.

Visit it, if you are in the area on the first Saturday or Sunday of the month. Pietra Ligure hosts a market at the corner of Piazza XX Settembre and Piazza La Pietra which combines crafts and antiques, trading on the last Saturday and Sunday of the month.

Victoria

Via Variante Aurelia, 96, Sarzana
Tel 01-87627190

For some, the greatest perk of visiting Italy is the opportunity to buy top designer fashion items at discounted prices.

Located near the northeastern border of La Spezia, the town Sarzana has an outlet that offers the designs of high-end labels such as Prada, Miu Miu and Hugo Boss at between 40 and 45 percent discount. The shop stocks men and women's clothing as well as a range of accessories and shoes.

Discounted Fashion Outlets

Euro Outlet - Genova
Via Guglielmo Marconi, 24 16010 Savignone
Tel: 010 9642862

This shop sells brands such as Dolce and Gabbana and Diesel at affordable prices.

Consorzio Portofranco Outlet - Genova
Via Sotto La Ripa, Tribogna 16030
Tel: 0185 939443

Browse here for a great selection of brands such as Guess, Nike, Prada, Dior, Dolce & Gabbana, Fendi and Gucci. Other great locations in Genoa to shop for discounted designer clothing includes the Fiumara Mall at Via San Luca and Via Caffa.

Cinque Terre

Cinque Terre (meaning "five lands" or "five castles") refers to the five villages of Riomaggiore, Manarola, Corniglia, Vernazza and Monterosso del Mar on the northwest coast of Italy. The five villages, which are connected by a hiking trail, draw 850,000 tourists each year yet are mostly unspoilt, continuing a lifestyle that goes back many generations.

The colorful houses in Cinque Terre cluster together on steep and craggy Mediterranean cliffs. Beautiful and picturesque, they seem married to the landscape. Here and there, the homes are interrupted by the presence of an ancient church or the remnants of a medieval castle.

Some village streets are lined by fishing boats. Other paths meander between terraced vineyards, lemon orchards and olive groves. In Italy's Cinque Terre, almost every road is worth travelling down (or up) for the amazing views.

The Cinque Terre is best experienced on foot and at a leisurely pace. There is no reason to rush. Nearly all of the streets are pedestrianized and the rhythm of village life is still determined by tide and season. As you pass through the vineyards and olive groves, you may experience a little of the heartbeat of rural Italy, seeing locals harvesting grapes or netting olive trees, depending on the time of year, using methods that are centuries old.

The villages of Cinque Terre remained relatively unknown to holidaymakers until the sixties. The hiking paths were first popularized by the guide book writer, Rick Steves, who remains intimately involved in promoting the region's potential. While the steep paths of Cinque Terre may be taxing to some, not all of Cinque Terre's walking routes are for hard-core hikers. The famous lover's walk or Via dell'Amore, which links Riomaggiore and Manarola, is a paved, even path that most should be able to master, and the scenery will be highly rewarding.

Cinque Terre is surrounded by the clear blue expanse of the Mediterranean Sea and conditions for sunbathing are ideal between May and October. Monterosso, the most tourist-oriented of the five, has a long sandy beach, with plenty of sunbeds and umbrellas that can be rented.

The beach at Vernazza is smaller, but offers beautiful views of the port area. At mealtimes, enjoy the fresh catch of the day, grilled to perfection with an excellent glass of local wine at one of the harborside trattorias, or, indulge your sweet tooth at one of the region's gelaterias, where you may enjoy one of a large selection of exotic flavors in an ice cream sandwich.

For a visit to Cinque Terre, travel as light as you can. Even if you will not be braving some of the more strenuous hiking trails, the beautiful hilltop location of all of the villages equates steep roads and many steps to get from one part of the village to another. Remember to bring hiking shoes, sunblock and plenty of bottled water. Be sure to pack a fully functional camera, too, as much of the area seems to be begging to be photographed.

Cinque Terre has a relaxed atmosphere, but despite its popularity with visitors, there are few hotels. Each of the villages has a culture and a dialect that is distinct, as they were only first linked in the early 20th century. Locals can tell, simply by listening to an individual's use of language, which village he or she is from. Most of the families living in the region go back many generations and they are proud of their traditions and heritage. Although tourism has evolved into an important part of the region's economy, many of the businesses are still locally owned and run.

Some of the villages, like Corniglia, go back to Roman times, but for many centuries, the existence was as precarious as the location. The inhabitants endured frequent raids by pirates and slave traders, evolving various survival strategies, such as homes with dual entrances. The Roman Catholic faith is the dominant religion, and certain religious festivals remain significant to the community.

The traditional cuisine of the region includes the focaccia, a simple flatbread made with olive oil and salt, the bruschetta and the farinata, baked from pepper, oil and chickpea meal. Pesto, made of basil leaves, a selection of cheeses, olive oil and garlic, is another local favorite. There are many places where you can buy cheap pesto as souvenir or gift. Olive oil features prominently in the cuisine, as does anchovies, which is often freshly caught, as well as various other types of seafood such as sea bass, swordfish, shrimp, lobster and clams. Walnuts are another local crop. Near the portside and beaches, you can expect to encounter an outlet or two that sells delicious gelato, often with mouth-watering varieties ranging from tiramisu, mango and berries to caramelized fig.

A famous Cinque Terre wine is Sciacchetrà which has a higher alcohol content than most wines. Besides wine, a favorite local drink is grappa, an aromatic type of brandy and limoncelo, a liqueur made from lemons. The poet Eugenio Montale was born in the Cinque Terre town of Monterosso and immortalized it in several of his poems.

Planning Your Stay

Cinque Terre refers to the five villages of Riomaggiore, Manarola, Corniglia, Vernazza and Monterosso del Mar on the northwest coast of Italy. The five villages, which are connected by a hiking trail, draw 850,000 tourists each year yet are mostly unspoilt, continuing a lifestyle that goes back many generations.

The nearest airports are Christoforo Colombo International Airport in Genoa and Galileo Galilei International Airport in Pisa. There is also a ferry service between the villages and from Genoa's Old Harbor, La Spezia, Lerici and Portovenere.

Cinque Terre is a mostly car-free zone, ideal for hiking, but with shuttle transport, a regular rail service and ferry boats available for transport. Driving between villages is not permitted. If you do plan to travel to the region by car, stop off in Riomaggiore, where the Autosilos garage would be willing to store your vehicle at a rate of €40 for two days. As much of the region relies on rail travel, the trains are much longer than the standard station platforms, meaning that often you can only get out via certain of the carriages of the train - usually the middle ones. Bear this in mind, to avoid missing your stop.

It is possible to hike from the nearby Portvenere, to the Cinque Terre village of Riomaggiore. The route is 13.5km and will take approximately six hours. The widest selection of hotel options are available in Monterosso, the largest and best developed of the five, but you may need to book in advance, especially in the popular summer season. The currency is the euro, but do bring cash, as ATMs are scarce and credit cards not always accepted. A good investment to make is the Cinque Terre card, which comes in three versions. The most basic one includes admission to various tourist spots, including the Cinque Terre National Park, as well as some transport allowances. The train card incorporates unlimited rail travel in the area, while the ferry card tops this up with unlimited access to the Cinque Terre ferry services.

Climate & Weather

Cinque Terre enjoys a Mediterranean climate, with the nearby mountains providing shelter against the impact of winds from the North. Summers are warm, with the closeness of the Mediterranean Sea contributing a moderating effect. Winters are cool, but rainy. By contrast, July is the driest month in Cinque Terre.

During July and August, day averages of up to 29 degrees Celsius can occur with night temperatures dropping to around 18 degrees Celsius.

During those months, a sea temperature of above 20 degrees Celsius can also be expected. June and September sees averages between 25 and 15 degrees Celsius, with May and October still enjoying day temperatures around 21 degrees Celsius and average night temperatures between 11 and 14 degrees Celsius. April temperatures, which average at around 17 degrees Celsius by day, might still be highly suitable for hiking, Cinque Terre's favorite activity. December, January and February are the coldest months with day averages between 11 and 12 degrees Celsius and night temperatures dropping to between 3 and 4 degrees Celsius. March and November sees day averages between 14 and 15 degrees Celsius and night averages between 6 and 7 degrees Celsius.

While the region displays some beautiful Nativity decoration during the winter time, most people are drawn to Cinque Terre for the hiking trails and these may not be open during late autumn or winter. For hikers, the region is great from as early as mid March right through to mid October and the best months for hiking are April, May, September and October, when temperatures are milder. Do remember that the heat at the height of summer may be scorching, if you are planning to put in a few hours of hiking every day. The summer months also tend to be the most crowded, in Cinque Terre. From mid October to November, the rainy season may result in some hiking trails being closed. If you are planning to spend most of your holiday sunbathing or enjoying other water activities, you will find the climate ideal from late May through to September.

As a result of its higher location, Corniglia tends to be slightly cooler than the rest of the villages. Although snow does not occur, the winter can see heavy rainfall, with the risk of landslides.

Sightseeing

Riomaggiore

Riomaggiore probably dates back to the 8th century, when settlers from the Vara Valley were drawn by a mild climate that proved ideal for the cultivation of grapes and olives.

It is the eastern most village of Cinque Terre and the one that connects to nearby La Spezia. In fact, the village is named after the river Maggiore, which needs to be crossed to reach Cinque Terre from that direction.

It is located between two hills and a noteworthy feature of the residential architecture is that most of the narrow homes have two doors on parallel streets. This conveniently provided an option of escape in case of Saraccen raids, during the turbulent 15th and 16th century.

From the railway station and the wharf area, the main center of town can be reached through a tunnel. It is the starting point of the easiest and best known trail of Cinque Terre. The famous Via dell'Amore walking route begins from the rail station. The main and most central street is Via Colombo. The village has several quaint little shops worth exploring and offers parking space to visitors who came by car. There is an elevator that will take you from the station to the higher parts of the village. The simple, yet colorful houses of Riomaggiore provide an attractive backdrop. A path carved from the cliffs will take you to a charming pebble beach.

For the more adventurous, Riomaggiore offers cliff-jumping. The Mediterranean Sea is clear, with great visibility of possible obstacles below. Riomaggiore is also the best and indeed only suitable location around Cinque Terre for indulging in a spot of scuba diving. The village has a diving center, which includes trips to the Capo Montenegro underwater reserve in its itinerary. There are dives suitable for beginners and more experienced divers. Kayaking, snorkelling and boat trips can be arranged as well.

Church of Saint John the Baptist

Riomaggiore

The Church of Saint John the Baptist in Riomaggiore shows the strong influence of Italian architect and sculptor Benedetto Antelami on the ecclesiastic art and architecture of Northern Italy. Although built more than a hundred years after Antelami's death, the heritage is still evident in various features, particularly the facade which includes an inscription of the stylistic contribution by Antelami masters, as commissioned by Antonio Fieschi, the bishop of Luni. There are two Gothic portals, three naves, a square apse and a dome-sprite steeple. Particularly striking is the rose window, sculpted in white marble.

The church was originally built around 1340, but a collapse in the 1800s led to a large-scale renovation project between 1870 and 1871. The interior includes various beautiful paintings, including a portrayal of John the Baptist by Domenico Fiasella and a huge wooden crucifix by Antonio Maria Maragliano. There is also a mechanical organ dating back to 1851.

Other Churches & Devotional Sites

The Chapel of St Rocco and St Sebastian was built in 1480, in the aftermath of a plague to remember its victims and includes a triptych featuring the Virgin, the Son and the saints. It is located on a hilltop, right next to the castle. The Oratory of Santa Maria Assunta can be found in the heart of the village and dates back to the 15th to 16th century. There is a wooden Madonna, as well as triptych featuring the Madonna, the Christ, John the Baptist and Domenico.

Castle of Riomaggiore

The castle of Riomaggiore dates back to 1260, when construction began under the Marquis Turcotti. The building project was completed under the Republic of Genoa and served as defensive structure against Barbarian raids. There are two circular towers in the boundary wall and the entrance is located between the two. The castle provides a brilliant view of the sea, as well as the Azure trail. There are benches to relax and a cemetery, which had been incorporated into the design. A steep road from Riomaggiore's railway station leads to the castle and it is open to the public.

Manarola

The village of Manarola is characterized by steep alleys and colorful housing. When passing through the tunnel to the train station of Manarola, spare a thought for the villagers who sheltered here during World War Two. The harbor is modest, but includes a ramp for boats. It is customary to pull the boats up onto the streets, in times of turbulent seas. Although Manarola has no beach to speak of, it does offer great deep water swimming potential. Fishing and wine are the main industries of the village.

Piazza Capellini, the town square, was laid out in 2004 and it soon became a relaxing spot to indulge the leisurely art of people watching. It offers great harbor views and features a colorful mosaic depicting various forms of marine life. The main street in the village is Via Discovolo.

There is a Cinque Terre travel office near the station. Manarola marks the beginning or end - depending on your personal perspective - of the world famous Via dell'Amore or Lovers' Walk, the most popular of all Cinque Terre's hiking trails. Via dell'Amore connects Manarola to its neighbour, Riomaggiore. Another fairly undemanding route is the Vineyard Walk, which begins just below the church and leads around the upper part of the village, where you can enjoy the soothing and fragrant presence of rosemary, red valerian and lemon trees. Interestingly, the road was once a river bed. For a scenic bonus, visit the nearby cemetery on Punto Bonfiglio.

One of the village's newer attractions is the Calandra Art Gallery (http://www.calandraarte.it/) which was founded in 1999. It focusses mainly on modern and contemporary art, and includes work in a variety of media and themes. The paintings of Claudio Ciardi realistically capture the scenery of Cinque Terre, while the creations of Francesco Nesi can be described as flights of fancy based on the unique landscape. Others, such as the work of Giuliano Ghelli, are more symbolic in nature. Calandra Art Gallery is located on Via A. Discovolo.

Church of San Lorenzo

A cornerstone from the facade dates the construction of the Church of San Lorenzo at 1338. The church is dedicated to the Nativity of the Virgin Mary and also San Lorenzo, the patron of the village. There is an impressive rose window, which was completed in 1375. The relief sculpture decorating the arch portal depicts the story of San Lorenzo. The square bell tower once served a defensive function.

The interior has Baroque features and by the main altar, you can admire a triptych with the Madonna and child, Saint Catherine and Saint Lorenzo. There is a second triptych of Saint Lorenzo, Saint Dominic and Saint John the Baptist. Most of the decorative work is by regional artists. The church itself is a fine example of Ligurian Gothic architecture as interpreted by the masters of Antelami and a foremost tourist attraction in Manarola. Most people do not visit Cinque Terre in winter, but if you happen to be around between 8 December and the end of January, you may be delighted to observe the biggest nativity display in the world, which includes 12,000 lamps and over 200 figures.

Corniglia

Corniglia may be be the oldest of the Cinque Terre villages and probably dates back to Roman times when its original name, *Gens Cornelia* alluded to the main family running village affairs. Unlike the other four, it has no harbour, but is instead located at an altitude of about 100m above sea level. The town is accessed through the Lardarina, a series of steps consisting of 33 flights and 382 individual steps.

Corniglia has approximately 300 permanent residents. Its main road is Via Fieschi, a street that winds past the bulk of its bars and shops, extending from the Church of San Pietro to St Mary's terrace. The street is named after Nicol Fieschi, a 13th century landowner. Administratively, the village falls under its neighbor, Vernazza. Thanks to its elevated position, it is possible to see panoramic views of all the other villages from Corniglia. The architecture of this village is a little different from the other four. Buildings are a little wider, as one would expect in inland settlements.

Corniglia is surrounded by terraced vineyards and its main industry is the cultivation of wine. If you look around, you may be fascinated by various little examples of medieval technology that were originally devised by the inhabitants to deal with the challenge of practicing agriculture on its steeply inclined terraces. For a uniquely close experience of rural Corniglia, why not consider a cosy stay at Barrani, one of its farms located at via Fieschi, 14.. There are fourteen beds available for visitors and breakfast will include freshly baked bread or rolls. Accommodation begins at about €45, but half board and weekly rates are available.

The scenic hamlet of Prevo, which is located halfway between Corniglia and Vernazza, offers a beautiful vantage point along the trail between the two villages.

The region is characterized by terraced olive groves and vineyards. Cinque Terre is accessible by rail via Genoa and La Spezia. The station for Corniglia is not within the town, but at the rocky beach of Spiaggione.

Church of San Pietro

The Church of San Pietro is located in the highest part of the village. The present building dates back to 1334, but there is evidence that it was built on the foundation of an earlier church, possibly from the 11th century. It is a good example of Ligurian Gothic architecture.

The christening font is from the 12th century. The facade features a beautiful white marble rose window, that goes back to 1351 and the interior includes a Baroque style vault and a rich variety of ornate and colorful religious frescoes. There is a statue of St Peter, the patron saint of Corniglia. A religious ceremony occurs annually on the 29th of June, which follows a route from the Church of San Pietro to the terrace of Santa Maria. A traditional cake, *Torte dei Fieschi*, is prepared for the occasion.

Largo Taragio

The main square of Largo Taragio dates back to the 18th century. It features an ancient well, which is connected to natural springs and once provided the town's water supply. There is also a memorial for Fallen Soldiers from World War One. The terrace of Santa Maria offers a spectacular overview of the entire Cinque Terre region. There are various cafes along Largo Taragio where you can enjoy a leisure lunch in a scenic environment. Bordering the square is the Oratory of the Disciplinati of Saint Catherine.

Oratory of the Disciplinati of Saint Catherine

The Oratory of the Disciplinati of Saint Catherine dates back to the 18th century. Its ceiling dome is decorated to evoke the sky and from the rear, a spectacular view of the Mediterranean Sea below can be experienced.

San Bernardino

The shrine of Our Lady of Grace (Nostra Signora delle Grazie), which dates back to 1800, is located in the tiny village of Bernardino, just above Corniglia. It features artwork depicting the Madonna and Child. At the plaza by the church, a modest cableway used mainly by wine growers, commences. San Bernardino offers brilliant sea views.

Guvano Beach

Although Corniglia offers no direct access to the coast, there is a beautiful, but secluded beach located halfway between Corniglia and Vernazza. This is Guvano Beach, a sheltered beach for nudists. It can be reached via a pedestrian tunnel and admission of €5 is charged. You may need to ring a buzzer to gain access and be sure to stock up on refreshments beforehand, as there are no vendors on the beach itself.

Vernazza

First established around 1000 AD, Vernazza fell under the rule of the Republic of Genoa from 1276. It has the only proper harbor of the Cinque Terre and much of the town's commercial and social activity is focussed around the harbor area. The nearby castle of Belforte has provided protection from the 1500s. The port is surrounded by a tightly clustered array of picturesque, pastel-colored houses, making it easy to see why it is regarded as one of the most beautiful villages in Italy. It has a permanent population of between 600 and 1000 inhabitants. There is a weekly market on Tuesdays.

The piazza is flanked by various restaurants and bars. Surrounded by terraced olive groves, the village is well known throughout Italy for the quality of its olive oil. Vernazza has a small, sandy beach, but the surrounding rocks are also popular with sunbathers. Although the town suffered considerable damage with the floods of 2011, the devastation led to a large-scale beautification enterprise, which added new paving from locally mined stone and various benches.

Voluntourism in Vernazza

http://savevernazza.com/

In 2011, floods and a devastating mudslide wreaked havoc and damage to the region. Out of the destruction, a unique community venture was born that serves to educate, enlighten and involve visitors to Vernazza.

For an in-depth guided excursion of Vernazza, consider getting involved with the Save Vernazza initiative. The purpose of the tour is to provide visitors with more insight into the culture, community and everyday life of Vernazza. Save Vernazza is a privately funded enterprise with various objectives, including architectural restoration, the fitting of energy efficient facilities and the addition of numerous items such as street benches, to encourage informal social interaction. The initiative also includes a voluntourism project, which allows visitors to help with community activities such as the harvesting of grapes, the restoration of terraces and the construction of dry stonewalls. For a donation of €30, which goes towards the project, participants will enjoy a guided tour, a work session where they will be able to interact with locals as well as a picnic lunch with some regional wine.

Monterosso del Mar

Monterosso divides into two distinct sections - the historical Old Town and its up-to-date sibling, the modern resort of Fegina, which may seem slightly reminiscent of the Italian Riviera. A pedestrian tunnel links the two.

Monterosso has the only sandy beach of the Cinque Terre region, with sunbathers having the option of renting an umbrella with chair, or settling in the free area with their own beach towels. In this village, you can expect the closest approximation of a tourist resort. The summertime vibe can get quite lively and may include a beach party of two. Bear in mind, though, while the town is busy by Cinque Terre standards, it is still fairly relaxed, if compared to more developed resorts. Various boat tours can be booked from Monterosso.

There are several night spots worth a visit. The trendy La Cantina di Miky offers live entertainment and a good selection of Italian beer, cocktails and grappa. Along Via Roma, there are numerous bars and restaurants. For your internet and other business and communication related needs, visit The Net at 55 Via Vittorio Emanuele in Monterosso del Mar. Enoteca Internazionale (http://www.enotecainternazionale.com/), at 61 Via Roma, is the town's original wine shop, which stocks over 500 different wines from all over Italy as well as distilled liquors.

Il Gigante

Via IV Novembre 11, 19016 Monterosso al Mare

The bay of Monterosso del Mare is watched over by an impressive 14m statue of Neptune.

Made of iron and concrete, it is the work of the Jewish-Italian artist Arrigo Minerbi and its striking presence right by the beach of Monterosso continues to impress and intrigue visitors. The sculpture was first installed in 1910 and withstood wartime bombardment during World War Two. It did lose an arm and a trident, though. The statue is located on Fegina Beach. On its shoulders, it carries the terrace of an Art Nouveau villa.

Monastery of the Capuchin Friars of Monterosso del Mar

Tel: 0187 817531
http://www.conventomonterosso.org/

According to the history of the region, the Capuchin monastery of Monterosso came to be as a gesture of gratitude. At the time, the religious community was split by a bitter feud, but a visit from two Capuchin friars resolved this and restored harmony to the warring factions. A cross was erected in 1618 and its church was consecrated and dedicated to St Francis of Assisi in 1623. In later years, the building was seized under Napoleon and again claimed during the first Reign of Italy in the 1860s. It fell into decay, but was re-purchased by a local priest, Don Giuseppe Policardi, from his savings. When he died, he bequeathed it to the original owners, the Capuchin friars.

The Capuchin monastery of Monterosso del Mar is worth a visit, if you are interested in Baroque painting. It features 'The Crucifixion', a painting attributed to the Flemish artist Anthony van Dyck, who was later a favorite painter of the court of Charles I of England. There is also a marble triptych by Domenico Gare, as well as works by the Ligurian artists Luca Cambiaso, Bernardo Strozzi, Agostino Ratti, Giuseppe Palmieri and Bernardo Castello. Don Policardi lies buried at the feet of the altar. Today, the monastery hosts a variety of activities such as concerts, seminars, art exhibitions and charitable events. It is open to the public and guided tours can be arranged.

Dawn Tower (Torre Aurora)

During the 16th century and before, the coast of Italy suffered frequent attacks from North Africa. Monterosso endured a devastating raid in 1545, which saw a number of houses being burnt down and women and children kidnapped to be sold as slaves. This led to a defensive system that included walls and various towers. Of these, only remnants remain.

The Dawn Tower is located between the hill of Saint Christoforo and the sea and also serves as a kind of boundary marker between the Old Town of Monterosso and the more commercialized Fegina resort section. It has been converted to a private home. Admission is €1.50.

Hiking in Cinque Terre

The Blue Trail (Trail Number 2)

The most popular of the longer routes is the Sentiero Azzurro, also known as the Blue Route or Trail number 2. This is a trail composed of four paths linking each of the five villages of Riomaggiore, Manarola, Corniglia, Vernazza and Monterosso. In 1999, the trail became part of the Cinque Terre National Park, which means that admission is charged and that the route is closed at night.

You can start the trail either from Riomaggiore or Monterosso. Although the super-active hiker may complete the whole route in about six hours, most visitors prefer to take a few days over it, pausing to explore the individual charms of each of the villages. This would give you the opportunity to explore each of the villages and enjoy some traditional snacks and wine before moving on.

Via Dell'Amore

The first part of the route, from the Riomaggiore side, is Via Dell'Amore, the popular lover's walk linking Riomaggiore to its nearest neighbor, Manarola. The trail is paved, and by far the easiest portion of the route. There is an interesting history to the establishment of this path.

Initially the villages of Cinque Terre were isolated, even from each other. Villagers rarely mixed. It all changed when the arrival of rail travel led to the creation of the first path between Riomaggiore and Manarola in the 1920s.

In the early days, there were frequent landslides, but interaction between inhabitants from the two villages increased and the path soon became a favorite meeting spot for young couples. Inscriptions of undying love can still be seen along the route, some dating back decades. There is also a tradition for lovers to leave a padlock along the route particularly below the tunnel on the Manarola side, as a physical token, locking their devotion to each other. The tradition is popular in Italy, particularly after it featured in a contemporary Young Adult novel. If you wish to partake, the special padlocks are sold at a hardware shop beside Bar Centrale, in Riomaggiore.

Approximately halfway between the two villages, you will encounter Bar dell'Amore. The building initially housed a gunpowder warehouse, but today it provides a scenic refreshment spot for walkers and hikers. The cafe serves, wine, cocktails and coffees as well as light snacks such as muffins and sandwiches. This section of the Blue Trail is 850m and takes approximately 20 minutes, although, with the spectacular scenery, you may wish to linger a little while longer.

From Manarola to Monterosso

Depending on which direction you come from, travelling to Corniglia, the highest of the five villages, will involve a fair amount of climbing. The route between Manarola and Corniglia takes about one hour. It is unpaved, steeper and somewhat narrower than the Via dell'Amore.

The trail between Corniglia and Vernazza is not particularly steep itself, but narrows to pass between two terraces with impressively sharp inclines. If you have over-estimated your stamina levels, you may be pleased to discover an emergency call facility, located between Corniglia and Vernazza.

The route from Vernazza to Monterosso del Mar is the longest of the four paths between the villages. It takes about two hours to complete and includes a fair amount of climbing both up and down before you reach your end destination. Admission of €5 is charged to walk this route.

The Five Sanctuaries Trail

One of the more unusual routes to hike through Cinque Terre is the Five Sanctuaries trail, which links to five spiritual landmarks, one for each of the villages. The route begins in Riomaggiore and travels upwards towards the Sanctuary of Montenero. The route is 3.5km and takes about one hour. There is a longer, more scenic route that runs parallel to the Riomaggiore canal, and then passes amongst the vineyards.

According to legend, a Byzantine icon was hidden here, to protect it from King Rotari of the Longobards. When it was recovered, a miraculous gushing of water lent the site religious significance and the sanctuary was built in 1335. The sanctuary was restored at various times and includes an 18th century fresco painted by Battaglia of Castelnuovo Magra.

The second part of the route will take you from Manarola's car park to the tiny village of Volastra, located halfway between Manarola and Corniglia. It is also a one hour route. Here you will find the Sanctuary of Our Lady of Health in Manarola. Its Romanesque design includes a pointed arch of sandstone and a Gothic style double lancet window.

The route from Corniglia to Our Lady of Graces is slightly longer. It passes the scenic lookout point, Prevo and becomes fairly steep towards the end. The sanctuary is associated with Bernardino da Siena, a Franciscan reformer from the 15th century. The sanctuary features a painting of the Madonna with Child.

Reaching Vernazza, you will travel from the rail station upwards to the Sanctuary of Our Lady of Reggio, located 300m above sea level. The trail is about 1.2km and will take about 45 minutes. The sanctuary dates back to the 11th century, but includes a crypt from an earlier structure. It includes the adored image of Madonna Nera with child, which is sometimes also referred to as the 'African'.

The final segment of the route is the longest. It begins at the end of Via Roma and passes through olive groves and vineyards before reaching the Sanctuary of Our Lady of Soviore. It is 2.5km and will take approximately an hour a half, but there is the more leisurely option of taking the bus.

The Sanctuary of Our Lady of Soviore is the oldest in Liguria and dates back to 643, when it sheltered the residents of former village of Albareto. In 996, it was honored with the presence of an emperor, Ottone III. The structure had seen numerous restoration efforts and retains elements of Romanesque, Gothic and Baroque architecture. The adored image is a wooden statue of the Pietà, dating back to the 15th century.

Cinque Terre High Trail (Trail Number 1)

Route 1 is also known as the High Route, and the complete trail extends from Levanto to Portovenere, covering 40km. It is estimated to take between 10 and 12 hours and passes along the ridge that separates the coastal settlements from the interior, through Colla di Gritta, Drignana, Cigoletta, La Croce and Telegrafo. None of The Five are visited, but if you are willing to brave the sometimes strenuous climbing, panoramic views of Cinque Terre will be your reward. The High Trail is recommended for experienced hikers and it may be best not to attempt the entire trail in one day. It is possible to connect to segments of the route, via sub trails.

Wine Tour of Cinque Terre

Because of the unusual landscape, with vineyards often occupying steep terraces, agricultural machinery is out of the question and most Cinque Terre vineyards are worked through manual labour. There is a system of monorails that can be used to haul harvested grapes to the nearest roads. Nevertheless, the ideal location of the region has allowed for great distribution of its wines, through Genoan maritime trade.

Cinque Terre is known for its dry whites. Farmers tend to grow crops of Bosco, Vermentino and Albarola grapes. The resulting wines are known for their delicate bouquet matched by a crisp acidity factor. The terroir of Cinque Terre D.O.C produces a taste that is very recognizable to experts. A local vintage worth sampling is Sciacchetrà, fairly sweet when young, although it exhibits a drier mouth when matured. At an alcohol content of 18 per cent, it is quite a bit stronger than most traditional wines, which is achieved by drying the grapes first for a few months.

If you want to experience the wine culture of Cinque Terre up close, why not book your accommodation at a wine farm. Buranco (http://www.burancocinqueterre.it/EN/agriturismo.html) at Via Buranco 72, Monterosso del Mare allows you to enjoy the natural rural splendor of Cinque Terre on a wine estate that also produces grappa, limoncino liqueur, honey and olive oil.

Meals include regional specialities and, of course, there is plenty of opportunity for wine tasting. Although the wine farm offers a tranquil environment, it is just a short walk from the town center and the beach of Monterosso. If you do not want to stay here, you can still visit to sample some of the wine and other produce.

Another type of wine tasting experience can be booked at A Pie de Ma, at Viale Giovanni Amendola in Riomaggiore. Here you can sample a selection of wines matched with the local cuisine. For €20, three wines are included, while a selection that includes each of the five villages will cost €33.

Recommendations for the Budget Traveller

Shopping

If you are looking for high-end fashion boutiques, Cinque Terre is not the best place. Most shops are small and quaint, selling the local wines, pastas, and pesto. There are also some craftsmen and women who create their own pottery and jewelry, allowing for tourists to take home a personal piece of Cinque Terre.

Cantina du Sciacchetra

Via Roma 7, 19016 Monterosso al Mare, Italy
(+39) 0187 817828

Cantina du Sciacchetrà sells wines, pesto, limoncello, and of course the local dessert wine, Sciacchetrà. The owners offer very friendly service with sampling provided. This is not only a good spot for shopping but also for packing a picnic to take with you to your terrace for a private lunch.

Enoteca Internazionale

62, Via Roma, Monterosso al Mare, Italy
(+39) 0187 817278
http://www.enotecainternazionale.com/enoteca-en.html

Enoteca Internazionale is the oldest wine shop in Monterosso, located in the old part of town.

Managed by the Barbieri family, the establishment proudly offers a wide variety of not only local Italian wines, but also international wines and liquors. Other local products such as pesto and olive oil are also sold but their claim to fame is through their wine sampling and knowledge of the wines. It is possible to arrange a tasting by reservation, when Enoteca Internazionale's professional sommeliers share their extensive knowledge with both groups and individuals.

Enoteca Sotto l'Arco

70, Via Roma, Vernazza, Italy
(+39) 0187 812124
info@enotecasottolarco.it
http://www.enotecasottolarco.it/

Enoteca Sotto l'Arco is located in Vernazza and is another establishment that offers visitors the opportunity to sample the local flavors of the Cinque Terre region. This is a popular shop amongst tourists, offering olive oils, pesto sauce, and pastas. You can feel free to purchase a bottle of wine at the shop, where the owners will open it for you and even give you cups to take to the piazza for enjoyment.

Il Mercante d'Oriente

Via Roma 8, Vernazza, Italy
(+39) 0187 812122

Also located in Vernazza is a shop called, Il Mercante d'Oriente. Right on the main street, Via Roma, it is located across from the pizzeria and offers a variety of crafts suitable for quality souvenirs. Authentic and handmade Italian jewelry can be found here, as well as beautiful, handcrafted scarves.

Galleria D'Arte Schiaccheart

Via S. Giacomo, 51, 19017 Riomaggiore
(+39) 0187 760056
info@sciaccheart.com

The Galleria D'Arte Schiaccheart is located in Riomaggiore and provides something to do for art lovers who may just enjoy window-shopping or who care to purchase something to take home from their visit in Cinque Terre. The gallery showcases contemporary art while giving opportunities for emerging artists to showcase their work. In the gallery, you will see paintings and also sculptures, ceramics, gifts, and jewelry.

The gallery is open Mondays through Saturdays from 10:30 until 13:00 and then again from 14:30 until 19:00. They are closed on Sundays.

Places to Stay

Cinque Terre is unique in its available accommodations. Choices range from traditional hotels in Monterosso to simple rooms and rented apartments in the rest of the four villages, known as "camere." You will find that rates are quite affordable when compared to the rest of Europe and the United States and often come with kitchens, private entryways, and breathtaking views. Keep in mind, however, with the views comes many steps through narrow passageways. Luggage with wheels does not help very much in Cinque Terre: it is muscles you will need to use - but it will be well worth the effort.

Many of the B&B's and camere (rooms) ask for cash upon arrival: do not assume they will accept credit cards. This should be mentioned at the time of booking, however, and should not come as a surprise. The few hotels that do exist may accept credit cards however. It is always wise to book in advance, especially during the summer months.

Hotel Villa Steno

Via Roma, 109-19016
Monterosso al Mare
(+39) 0187 817028
http://www.villasteno.com/en/

Monterosso's Hotel Villa Steno is a quaint, 16 room, family-run hotel situated in the middle of Monterosso's old town.

It is a brief four minute walk from the beach and hiking path that leads to the other towns of Cinque Terre. Guests appreciate the best of both worlds, as they are treated to both a lovely view of the sea as well as a view of Monterosso's old town. The location is quiet, surrounded by citrus and olive trees.

All rooms have been recently remodeled with 14 of them offering either a balcony or small private garden with a view of either the sea or the old town. Each room has a private bathroom with shower, hairdryer, safe, telephone, television, refrigerator, and air conditioning.

Although rates are on the higher end for Cinque Terre, they are still affordable for the budget traveler who wants a good value at between €120 and €200 for a double room.

La Marina Rooms

Various Locations
Vernazza, Italy
(+39) 338 47 67472
mapcri@yahoo.it
http://www.lamarinarooms.com/

Owner Christian Carro takes great care of his four available rentals. There is a single room, two double rooms, and an apartment overlooking the sea. He is very helpful and prompt with emails and phone calls. Prices range from €60 for a single room to €130 for the apartment – an incredible value considering you get a furnished kitchen, two large bedrooms and arguably the best private terrace in Vernazza with an amazing sea view.

Il Carugio di Corniglia

Via alla Stazione 19, 19018, Corniglia, Italy
http://www.ilcarugiodicorniglia.com/
Tel: (+39) 0187 81 22 93
Cell: (+39) 335 17 57 946
Cell: (+39) 339 22 83 803
info@ilcarugiodicorniglia.com

Rooms (camere) and apartments in Corniglia are situated on its main street, called the Carugio.

Taking its name from the street is Il Carugio di Corniglia, offering several options for accommodations. Il Carugio offers a panoramic terrace with tables, chairs, and a fantastic view over Corniglia, the sea, vineyards, and Sanctuary of San Bernadino.

There is a bus that runs from the rail station up the steep incline to the village: be sure to consider using it, especially if you are toting heavy luggage. Rates vary, but are appealing to the budget conscious traveler. Be sure to contact the hotel directly for accurate rates.

Arpaiu

Via Belvedere 196, 19010 Manarola, Italy
(+39) 340 687 9732
info@arpaiu.com
http://www.arpaiu.com/english.html

People come to Manarola of all the five villages when they are looking for romance. Arpaiu definitely succeeds in providing a romantic ambiance.

There are four rooms to choose from, as well as an apartment with kitchenette that accommodates three people. All have water views and either a shared or private terrace. Service is impeccable and friendly. There are several stairs leading to the property but it is worth the climb for those who are capable. All rooms provide satellite TV, a safe, a mini bar, a hair dryer, private bathrooms, and wireless internet.

Rates range between €90 and €130.

Alla Marina

Via San Giacomo 61, 19017 Riomaggiore, Italy
(+39) 328 013 4077
info@allamarina.com
http://www.allamarina.com/index-eng.php?lang=en

An affordable and much-loved vacation rental in Riomaggiore is Guest house "Alla Marina." Perched right upon the sea, it offers three separate rooms, two of which have sea views. In 2011, the guest house was completely renovated, offering modern conveniences like Wi-Fi, as well as a private bathroom, safe, and mini bar in each room. A small breakfast is included in the rate and is provided in each room.

Alla Marina offers free parking to those who have traveled by car, since Riomaggiore is the southernmost village and is reachable by car. If traveling by train, it is only a four-minute walk from the train station to the residence.

The room rates are €120 for two people and €135 for three. The Atlantis Apartment, which has a private terrace with two bedrooms and two bathrooms, costs €180.

Eating & Drinking

The food and wine of the Cinque Terre are a great attraction for "foodies" who love fresh seafood and pasta. A local specialty of Cinque Terre is the accuighe, pronounced (ah-CHOO-gay). To English speakers, these are known as anchovies. They are often served the day they are caught, right off the shores of the villages. These are not the salted, canned anchovies often seen in the United States: they are served in olive oil and lemon juice, plump, delicious, and unrecognizable to those expecting the anchovies often seen on pizza. The region is also the birthplace of pesto, so be sure to sample it as well.

The local wine of Cinque Terre (Vino delle Cinque Terre) is an inexpensive but delicious white wine served throughout the region. It pairs well with seafood, not too sweet and not too dry. Its Sciacchetrà is a more expensive dessert wine that is local to the region. Locals can be seen dipping their biscotti in it and sipping it from delicate, small glasses.

Enoteca da Eliseo (Wine Bar)

3 Piazza Matteotti, Monterosso al Mare, Italy
(+39) 0187 817308

Enoteca da Eliseo is a small, charming, family-run wine bar that serves up friendliness and a particular ambiance along with its wine. The prices are affordable, the drink menu is extensive, and the owners are accommodating. Along with the wine samples is served caper berries, olives, and peanuts. This is not a restaurant: only a wine bar, but one of the best in the region. Situated in the old town, it offers imbibers a chance to enjoy a before or after dinner drink on the cobblestone streets of Monterosso.

Il Casello

Via Corone, Monterosso al Mare, Italy
(+39) 0187 818330

Monterosso's Il Casello offers a casual atmosphere with good food that utilizes fresh, local produce. The beach view should not go unmentioned. They only accept cash, so be prepared to keep your credit cards in your wallet. The prices are affordable when compared to other beachside restaurants.

Il Pirata delle Cinque Terre

Via G Guidoni, 36, Vernazza, Italy
(+39) 0187 812047
http://www.ilpiratarooms.com/eng_home.html

Not only does Il Pirata della Cinque Terre offer fantastic meals for breakfast, lunch, and dinner; they also offer conversation and genuine friendliness of two brothers who absolutely love their jobs and are proud of their heritage.

Often times tourists come back simply to say hello and have a coffee, even sending postcards from home which are proudly displayed on the walls of the establishment. Massimo and Gianluca are twin brothers from Sicily who serve delicious food and pastries which are displayed inside.

Il Pirate della Cinque Terre is not situated in the busy harbor with the other restaurants. Instead, it sits near the train station above the rest of town. Have a seat outside, along the stream and homes of locals. Prices are affordable for what is often considered a favorite meal by tourists. They also offer rooms which can be viewed on their website.

Marina Piccola's Ristorante Albergo Sul Mare

Via Lo Scalo, 16, 19010 Manarola, Italy
(+39) 0187 920923
http://www.hotelmarinapiccola.com/ristorante/en

Also a hotel in Manarola, the Marina Piccola's restaurant - Ristorante Albergo Sul Mare - offers a fantastic fresh seafood menu. Chefs create dishes that rely on what is in season at the time, to guaranty only the freshest and highest quality ingredients. The fantastic view complements the food as well. Prices start at €10 ($13) and depend upon the expense of the seafood that day.

Il Borgo di Campi

Via Litoranea, Riomaggiore, Italy
(+39) 0187 760111
http://www.borgodicampi.it/

Also a hotel in Riomaggiore, the restaurant offers visitors the chance to taste local meat and seafood dishes at a more affordable price than its neighboring restaurants. They also create their own Sciacchetrà (dessert wine), olive oils, biscuits, pestos, and other Ligurian sauces. Il Borgo di Campi offers a sea-view terrace for its guests, creating a delightful ambience surrounded by thyme, marjoram, and rosemary plants.

ITALIAN RIVIERA & CINQUE TERRE TRAVEL GUIDE

Printed in Great Britain
by Amazon